Rekindling Love

Lessons from Penguins and Faith

to Restore Your Marriage

By Albert Barzaga

Table of Contents

Introduction: A Love That Withstands the Cold

In the frigid landscapes of the Antarctic, a remarkable story unfolds each year: the courtship and commitment of the penguin. These remarkable creatures, with their unwavering loyalty and steadfastness, serve as a profound illustration of love's resilience in the harshest conditions. Just like the penguins, many couples face the chilling winds of life that can freeze their affections and distance their hearts. Yet, within these icy trials lies the promise of rekindling the warmth that once ignited their relationship.

In our fast-paced, often cold society, it's all too easy for love to grow cold. The stresses of daily life, misunderstandings, and the pressures of the world can create an emotional distance that seems insurmountable. But what if we could learn from the penguins? What if we could draw on the wisdom inherent in God's creation to restore the fire of our love?

This book is a journey of rediscovery, drawing powerful parallels between the tenacity of penguins and the sacred bond of marriage. We will explore how God designed these incredible birds to embody qualities that can guide us in overcoming the challenges we face as partners. Through faith and reflection, we can reignite the love that may have waned and build a relationship that thrives, even in the coldest of circumstances.

Each chapter will offer insights into the nature of commitment, the strength found in unity, and practical steps to foster a deeper connection. You will find biblical principles intertwined with the lessons we can learn from our feathered friends, offering hope and direction as you navigate the path to rekindling love in your marriage.

As you embark on this journey, remember: love is not a fleeting emotion but a choice we make every day. Just as the penguins huddle together to survive the harsh winter, we too can choose to draw closer to one another, igniting the warmth of love that God intended for us. Let us dive into the profound wisdom found in creation, and may this book inspire you to embrace the beauty of rekindling love in your marriage.

Prepare to be transformed, for a renewed love story awaits you—one that mirrors the enduring commitment of penguins and the unchanging love of God. Together, let's thaw the coldness that may have settled into your relationship and uncover the vibrant warmth that lies beneath. Welcome to a journey of hope, healing, and rekindled love.

Chapter 1: Embracing God's Design in Penguins and Marriage

In the icy realms of the Antarctic, where temperatures plummet and survival is a daily challenge, penguins thrive through a remarkable bond. They huddle together, providing warmth and protection against the harsh climate. This instinctive behavior not only keeps them warm but also illustrates a fundamental truth about relationships: together, we can weather any storm.

Just as penguins are designed for commitment, so too are we, created in God's image, made for connection and love. In the Bible, we find the beautiful depiction of love in Genesis, where God creates companionship for Adam. He declares, "It is not good for the man to be alone" (Genesis 2:18). This divine design reflects a fundamental aspect of our humanity: we are meant to be in relationships that nurture and support us.

The Penguin's Journey: A Model of Commitment

Penguins are renowned for their loyalty. Once they find a mate, they embark on a journey together that involves courtship, nesting, and raising their young. During the breeding season, they perform elaborate mating dances, showcasing their commitment to one another. This commitment doesn't end after the eggs are laid; both partners share the responsibility of keeping the eggs warm and safe. They take turns watching over their young, exemplifying the power of teamwork and dedication.

In a marriage, this same spirit of commitment is crucial. When couples pledge to love each other, they embark on a journey that requires intentionality, mutual respect, and the willingness to face challenges together. Like penguins, we must recognize that our relationships thrive when we actively support one another.

God's Design for Partnership

God's design for marriage mirrors the penguin's partnership. In Ephesians 5:25-33, the Apostle Paul instructs husbands to love their wives as Christ loves the church. This sacrificial love requires an understanding of the depth of commitment and care. It is not merely an emotional bond; it is a covenant grounded in faith and devotion.

Consider how penguins instinctively protect and nurture their young. In doing so, they demonstrate the qualities of love, sacrifice, and responsibility. In our marriages, we are called to embody these same traits, nurturing each other's hearts and working together to build a family rooted in faith.

Building a Foundation of Commitment and Trust

To embrace God's design for marriage, we must first build a solid foundation of commitment and trust. This requires open communication and a willingness to be vulnerable. Just as penguins rely on each other for warmth, we must create an environment where both partners feel safe to express their thoughts and feelings.

1. **Practice Open Communication**: Set aside time to talk about your hopes, fears, and dreams. This practice not only strengthens your bond but also fosters understanding and empathy.
2. **Create Shared Goals**: Work together to establish common goals for your marriage and family. Whether it's planning a vacation, saving for a home, or nurturing your faith, shared aspirations can unite you.
3. **Support Each Other's Growth**: Just as penguins take turns nurturing their young, be supportive of each other's individual growth. Encourage one another to pursue passions and personal development.

4. **Pray Together**: Bringing God into your relationship is essential. Pray together for guidance, strength, and unity. This spiritual connection deepens your bond and aligns your hearts with His purpose.

As we explore the lessons from penguins and reflect on God's design for marriage, remember that love is an ongoing journey. It requires effort, grace, and a deep commitment to one another. By embracing the qualities that God instilled in His creation, we can cultivate relationships that not only endure but flourish.

In the chapters to come, we will delve deeper into the lessons from penguins, exploring how we can navigate life's challenges together, protect our love, and ultimately reignite the passion that may have cooled. Together, let us learn how to embrace God's design in our marriages and discover the warmth of love that can withstand even the coldest of winters.

Chapter 2: Surviving the Winter: Endurance Through Hard Times

Life is full of seasons, and just like the penguins endure the bitter cold of winter, so too do couples face challenging times that can test their love and commitment. In these moments, it's easy to feel isolated and distant, but remember that enduring the harshest winters together can ultimately strengthen your bond.

The Cold Winds of Life

The pressures of everyday life—work, financial stress, parenting, and external expectations—can create a frigid atmosphere in our relationships. These cold winds can cause misunderstandings, lead to resentment, and even drive a wedge between partners. Yet, just as penguins face the chill of winter together, we too can find ways to support and uplift each other during difficult times.

When a storm hits, penguins huddle closely, sharing warmth and protecting one another. This instinctive behavior serves as a powerful reminder that when we face adversity, drawing close to our partner is crucial.

Lessons from Penguins: Enduring the Storms Together

1. **Huddle for Support**: Just as penguins come together in a tight circle to conserve warmth, couples can benefit from seeking each other out during tough times. Make it a priority to spend quality time together, even amidst chaos. This can be as simple as having a quiet evening after a long day or a weekend getaway to reconnect.
2. **Communicate Openly**: In the coldest moments, it's essential to maintain open lines of communication. Share your feelings, fears,

and frustrations with your partner. By discussing your struggles, you create an atmosphere of trust, allowing both of you to express vulnerability without fear of judgment.

3. **Encourage Each Other**: During difficult times, words of encouragement can be a powerful source of strength. Remind each other of your love and commitment. Just as penguins take turns caring for their young, support each other's dreams and aspirations, even when life feels overwhelming.

Trusting God in the Midst of Marital Struggles

Throughout the storms of life, it's vital to lean on your faith. Trusting God not only helps you navigate the challenges but also reminds you of the greater purpose behind your struggles. In Romans 5:3-5, we read that suffering produces perseverance; perseverance, character; and character, hope.

Remember that God is always present in your relationship, even during the winter seasons. Lean into prayer together, asking for guidance and strength. Let your faith become the warm blanket that envelops you both, allowing you to face the cold winds with confidence.

Practical Steps to Foster Endurance

To endure the winter months in your marriage, consider implementing these practical steps:

1. **Create a Resilience Plan**: Discuss potential challenges you may face and create a plan together. Identify ways to support each other during tough times, whether it's managing finances or handling family conflicts.
2. **Set Aside Time for Each Other**: Amidst busy schedules, carve out intentional time for one another. This could be regular date

nights, shared hobbies, or simply moments of quiet reflection together.

3. **Reflect on Your Journey**: Take time to revisit the memories that brought you together. Share stories of your relationship and the obstacles you've overcome. This reflection can reignite gratitude and strengthen your resolve to face future challenges together.

4. **Seek Help When Needed**: Don't hesitate to seek support from trusted friends, family, or a counselor if needed. Just as penguins rely on their colony, so too should you lean on your support network.

By embracing these strategies, you can learn to navigate the cold winds of life together, turning challenges into opportunities for growth and deeper connection.

Conclusion: A Love That Grows Stronger

As you endure the winter seasons in your marriage, remember that love is a choice, and commitment is an active pursuit. Just as penguins demonstrate unwavering loyalty to one another, you too can choose to stand by your partner, even in the face of adversity.

The journey may not always be easy, but every challenge overcome together adds layers of strength to your relationship. In the next chapter, we will explore how to foster closeness and intimacy, drawing on the lessons learned from the penguins' survival in the cold. Together, let us continue to nurture the warmth of love, ensuring it burns brightly through every season of life.

Chapter 3: The Power of Unity: Staying Close Amid the Cold

As the winter winds howl and the temperatures drop, the bonds of penguins grow ever stronger. Their instinct to huddle together serves not only to conserve warmth but also to foster a sense of unity and safety. In our own relationships, cultivating a sense of closeness and partnership is essential for weathering life's challenges and nurturing the warmth of love.

Penguins Huddle for Warmth: The Importance of Intimacy

When penguins gather tightly in a huddle, they create a protective barrier against the elements, reminding us of the profound importance of intimacy in our relationships. This closeness isn't just physical; it encompasses emotional and spiritual connections as well. In a world that often promotes isolation, we must intentionally create spaces for vulnerability and support in our marriages.

Intimacy is more than just sharing physical space; it involves sharing thoughts, dreams, fears, and aspirations. This emotional closeness can act as a shield against the coldness that life can bring.

Biblical Unity: "Two Are Better Than One"

In Ecclesiastes 4:9-12, we find the powerful reminder that "Two are better than one, because they have a good return for their labor." This verse highlights the strength found in partnership. When we unite as a couple, we can achieve more than we could ever accomplish alone. This unity fosters not only resilience but also joy in our shared experiences.

Practical Steps to Enhance Closeness

1. **Prioritize Quality Time**: Schedule regular time together without distractions. This could be a weekly date night, a shared hobby, or even quiet moments to reflect and connect. Consistent quality time nurtures intimacy and strengthens your bond.
2. **Engage in Meaningful Conversations**: Make it a habit to discuss more than just the day-to-day logistics of life. Ask open-ended questions about each other's hopes and dreams. Listen actively, offering your full attention and understanding. This practice deepens emotional intimacy and creates a safe space for sharing.
3. **Express Affection**: Small gestures of love—hugs, kisses, holding hands—can significantly enhance feelings of closeness. Verbal affirmations of love and appreciation can also serve as powerful reminders of your commitment to one another.
4. **Pray Together**: Spiritual intimacy is a vital aspect of any marriage. Spend time in prayer together, asking for guidance, support, and unity. Sharing your spiritual journey can create a strong bond and foster deeper connections.

Protecting Each Other's Hearts

As penguins take turns caring for their young, we too must be intentional in protecting each other's hearts. This involves being aware of each other's feelings, needs, and vulnerabilities.

- **Encourage Open Communication**: Create an environment where both partners feel comfortable sharing their emotions. If something is bothering you, bring it up gently and constructively. This openness helps prevent misunderstandings and builds trust.
- **Practice Forgiveness**: Just as no relationship is perfect, conflicts and misunderstandings will arise. Make it a priority to forgive each other and move forward. Holding onto resentment only breeds distance, while forgiveness opens the door to healing.

- **Be Each Other's Advocate**: Stand up for each other, both in private and in public. Show support and loyalty, reinforcing the idea that you are a united front, no matter the challenges you face.

Conclusion: Building a Stronger Bond

As we navigate life together, remember that unity is a choice we make daily. By prioritizing intimacy, engaging in meaningful conversations, and supporting one another, we can create a safe haven for love to flourish.

In the next chapter, we will explore how to reignite the fire of passion in your marriage, drawing inspiration from the unwavering commitment of penguins. Together, we will discover ways to warm the hearts of one another and nurture the love that God intended for your relationship. Let us embrace the power of unity as we continue this journey of rekindling love.

Chapter 4: Rekindling the Flame: Igniting Passion in Your Relationship

As the long winter months wane, the penguins prepare for the arrival of spring—a season filled with renewal, life, and energy. This transformation serves as a beautiful reminder that love, like the changing seasons, can also be revitalized and reignited. In our relationships, nurturing passion and affection is essential to keep the flame of love burning bright.

Understanding the Essence of Passion

Passion is not just about physical intimacy; it encompasses emotional and spiritual connections as well. It involves a deep appreciation for one another, an eagerness to explore new experiences together, and a commitment to keeping the excitement alive. Just as penguins express their affection through bonding behaviors, couples must also find ways to connect on multiple levels.

Rediscovering What Draws You Together

One of the first steps to rekindling passion is to revisit the very things that brought you together in the first place. Reflect on the shared interests, adventures, and moments that ignited your connection.

- **Revisit Old Memories**: Go through photos or mementos that remind you of special moments in your relationship. Share stories about your favorite dates, vacations, or simply the early days of your romance. This reflection can reignite feelings of joy and nostalgia.
- **Engage in Shared Activities**: Explore activities you both enjoy or try something new together. Whether it's cooking, hiking, or

taking a dance class, engaging in shared experiences fosters connection and excitement.

Creating Opportunities for Intimacy

In the hustle and bustle of life, intimacy can sometimes take a backseat. However, making a conscious effort to create opportunities for closeness can make a significant difference.

1. **Date Nights**: Set aside dedicated time for each other. Plan regular date nights that allow you to reconnect without distractions. This could be a cozy dinner at home, a movie night, or an adventure exploring your city.
2. **Surprise Each Other**: Keep the spark alive by surprising your partner with small gestures. Leave a sweet note, prepare their favorite meal, or plan a spontaneous outing. These thoughtful actions show love and consideration, helping to reignite passion.
3. **Prioritize Physical Affection**: Physical touch plays a vital role in maintaining intimacy. Hold hands, cuddle on the couch, or give each other massages. These simple gestures can deepen your connection and remind you of your love for one another.

Fostering Emotional Connection

Beyond physical intimacy, fostering emotional connection is crucial for rekindling passion. Emotional safety creates an environment where both partners feel valued and understood.

- **Share Your Dreams**: Take time to discuss your dreams and aspirations, both individually and as a couple. Encouraging each other's goals fosters a deeper connection and allows you to grow together.

- **Practice Gratitude**: Express gratitude for each other regularly. Acknowledging the little things can strengthen your bond and create a positive atmosphere in your relationship.

The Role of Faith in Rekindling Love

In the journey to reignite passion, it's important to involve your faith. Bringing God into your relationship can deepen your connection and provide guidance as you navigate challenges.

- **Pray Together**: Spend time in prayer, asking God to renew your love and passion for one another. Seek His guidance in strengthening your relationship and igniting the flames of intimacy.
- **Study Scripture Together**: Explore passages that speak to love and relationships. Reflecting on God's design for marriage can inspire and guide you as you work to rekindle the passion in your relationship.

Conclusion: Embracing the Journey of Renewal

Just as the arrival of spring brings new life and vibrancy to the penguins' world, so too can we embrace the journey of renewal in our relationships. Rekindling the flame of passion requires intention, effort, and a willingness to explore the depths of love.

In the next chapter, we will delve into the importance of forgiveness and healing in maintaining a thriving relationship. Together, we will discover how letting go of past hurts can create space for a deeper, more passionate love to flourish. Let us commit to nurturing the love God intended for us, embracing the beauty of renewal in every season of life.

Chapter 5: The Healing Power of Forgiveness

In the harsh winters, even penguins face challenges that can lead to conflict and tension within their communities. However, they also demonstrate a remarkable ability to forgive and move forward. This chapter explores the vital role of forgiveness in healing relationships, allowing love to thrive once more.

Understanding the Importance of Forgiveness

Forgiveness is a powerful act that frees us from the burdens of resentment and anger. Holding onto past grievances can create a cold atmosphere in our relationships, stifling intimacy and connection. Just as penguins must work together to survive, couples must learn to forgive in order to foster a warm, loving environment.

The Weight of Unforgiveness

Unforgiveness can feel heavy, much like the weight of ice and snow on a penguin's back. It can create distance, misunderstandings, and even resentment. When we allow past hurts to linger, we hinder our ability to experience the fullness of love that God intends for us.

In Matthew 6:14-15, we learn about the importance of forgiving others as God forgives us. This principle serves as a reminder that forgiveness is not just for the benefit of the one who has wronged us, but also for our own spiritual and emotional well-being.

Steps Toward Forgiveness

1. **Acknowledge the Hurt**: Recognizing the pain caused by your partner's actions is the first step toward healing. It's important to express your feelings honestly, allowing both partners to understand the impact of the hurt.

2. **Choose to Forgive**: Forgiveness is a choice, often requiring intentional effort. Make the decision to let go of the past, even if it feels difficult. Remember that forgiveness does not mean condoning the behavior but choosing to release its hold on your heart.
3. **Communicate Openly**: Discuss the issues that led to the hurt in a calm and respectful manner. Sharing your feelings can foster understanding and pave the way for healing.
4. **Pray for Strength**: Turning to God in prayer can provide the strength needed to forgive. Ask for His guidance as you navigate the journey of healing and reconciliation.

The Role of Healing in Relationships

Healing takes time, much like the thawing of ice in spring. It is a process that requires patience and commitment from both partners. Here are some key aspects to consider:

- **Establish Trust Again**: After forgiveness, rebuilding trust is essential. Be transparent with one another, and take small steps to demonstrate your commitment to change and growth.
- **Create New Memories**: As you heal, focus on creating positive experiences together. Engaging in activities that bring joy and laughter can help reinforce your bond and create a fresh start.
- **Seek Professional Help if Needed**: Sometimes, past wounds can be deep, and seeking the guidance of a counselor can be beneficial. Professional help can provide tools and strategies for navigating complex emotions and rebuilding your relationship.

God's Forgiveness as a Model

As we strive to forgive our partners, it's important to remember the model of forgiveness that God provides us. In Ephesians 4:32, we are reminded to "be kind and compassionate to one another, forgiving each other, just as in Christ God forgave you." This divine perspective encourages us to approach forgiveness with grace and love, mirroring the compassion we receive from God.

Conclusion: The Freedom of Forgiveness

Forgiveness is a transformative act that can break the chains of hurt and resentment. By choosing to forgive, we create a space for healing, intimacy, and renewed love. Just as penguins thrive in their communities through cooperation and understanding, we too can flourish in our relationships by embracing forgiveness.

In the next chapter, we will explore the beauty of commitment and the vows we make to one another. Together, we will learn how to cultivate a lasting love that stands the test of time, reinforcing the bonds of marriage through every season of life. Let us embrace the healing power of forgiveness and allow our relationships to blossom once more.

Chapter 6: The Beauty of Commitment: Building a Lasting Love

As spring arrives, the penguins are not only focused on nurturing their young but also on reaffirming their commitment to one another. This steadfast loyalty is a testament to the strength of their bonds, providing a solid foundation for their family. In our relationships, commitment is equally vital; it creates stability, trust, and a safe haven for love to flourish.

Understanding Commitment in Marriage

Commitment is more than just a promise; it's a deep-seated intention to love and support one another through every season of life. It involves a conscious decision to prioritize your partner, even when challenges arise.

In Proverbs 3:3-4, we are encouraged to let love and faithfulness never leave us. This biblical perspective highlights the importance of nurturing our commitments and the blessings that come from doing so.

The Strength Found in Vows

When couples exchange vows, they create a sacred promise that signifies their intention to be together. These vows serve as a guiding light, reminding us of the love and dedication we have for one another.

- **Renew Your Vows**: Consider setting aside time to renew your commitment to each other. This can be a simple ceremony or a heartfelt conversation where you express your love and intentions. Reflecting on your journey together can deepen your bond and reignite your shared purpose.

- **Live Out Your Vows Daily**: Commitment is a daily practice. Make a conscious effort to show love, respect, and kindness in your interactions. Small gestures, like leaving a sweet note or making time for a heartfelt conversation, reinforce your vows and keep the connection alive.

Cultivating Trust and Loyalty

Trust is a cornerstone of commitment. Without it, relationships can easily falter. Building trust takes time and effort, but it is essential for a strong partnership.

1. **Be Transparent**: Open communication fosters trust. Share your thoughts, feelings, and any concerns with one another. Honesty and vulnerability lay the groundwork for a solid foundation.
2. **Follow Through on Promises**: Keeping your word is crucial. When you make promises to your partner, strive to fulfill them. This builds reliability and shows that you value your commitment.
3. **Support Each Other**: Be each other's biggest cheerleaders. Celebrate successes and provide comfort during difficult times. Supporting one another strengthens your bond and reinforces your loyalty.

Embracing Change Together

As life unfolds, change is inevitable. Navigating life's transitions—whether they are personal, professional, or familial—requires a strong commitment to one another.

- **Adapt Together**: Embrace the changes in your lives as opportunities for growth. Work together to tackle challenges, understanding that you are stronger as a team.

- **Stay Connected**: In times of change, make a conscious effort to remain connected. Regularly check in with each other, share your thoughts, and adapt your plans as needed.

Faith as a Foundation for Commitment

Incorporating your faith into your relationship can greatly enhance your commitment. When you center your relationship around God, you create a strong foundation that supports both partners.

- **Pray for Guidance**: Regularly pray together, seeking God's wisdom in your journey. Invite Him into your relationship and ask for strength to uphold your commitments.
- **Reflect on Scripture**: Explore biblical teachings that emphasize commitment and love. Meditating on verses can provide encouragement and direction as you navigate your relationship.

Conclusion: Celebrating Lasting Love

Commitment is a beautiful gift that allows love to flourish in our relationships. By nurturing our vows, cultivating trust, and embracing change together, we can build a lasting love that withstands the test of time. Just as penguins support one another in raising their young, we too must support each other through life's challenges.

In the next chapter, we will explore the importance of communication in nurturing our relationships. Together, we'll discover how to express our needs, desires, and feelings in ways that strengthen our bonds and deepen our love. Let us celebrate the beauty of commitment and the love that it fosters in our lives.

Chapter 7: The Power of Communication: Nurturing Connection through Words

In the vibrant world of penguins, communication is essential. From the soft coos of courtship to the intricate dances that signal affection, these birds rely on a rich language to connect with one another. In our relationships, effective communication serves as the lifeline that keeps love alive, fostering understanding and connection between partners.

Understanding Communication in Relationships

Communication is more than just exchanging words; it involves sharing thoughts, feelings, and needs in a way that strengthens the bond between partners. When done well, communication builds trust and fosters emotional intimacy. However, poor communication can lead to misunderstandings and distance.

The Importance of Active Listening

One of the most crucial aspects of communication is active listening. This means fully engaging with your partner, giving them your undivided attention, and seeking to understand their perspective.

1. **Create a Safe Space**: Ensure that your conversations take place in a comfortable environment where both partners feel safe expressing their thoughts and emotions. This openness lays the groundwork for deeper discussions.
2. **Practice Empathy**: Strive to understand your partner's feelings and point of view. Respond with empathy and compassion, showing that you value their thoughts and emotions.
3. **Ask Open-Ended Questions**: Encourage deeper conversations by asking open-ended questions that invite your partner to share

more about their feelings and experiences. This can lead to meaningful discussions that strengthen your connection.

Expressing Your Needs and Desires

While listening is vital, expressing your own needs and desires is equally important. Honest communication about what you want and need from your partner can help prevent misunderstandings and resentment.

- **Use "I" Statements**: When discussing feelings, frame your statements using "I" to express your emotions without placing blame. For example, say, "I feel neglected when we don't spend time together," rather than "You never make time for me."
- **Be Clear and Direct**: Clearly articulate your needs and desires. Avoid vague language that can lead to confusion. The more direct you are, the easier it is for your partner to understand and respond.

Handling Conflict with Grace

Conflict is a natural part of any relationship. How we handle disagreements can significantly impact the strength of our connection. Here are some strategies for navigating conflict gracefully:

1. **Stay Calm**: Approach conflicts with a calm demeanor. Take deep breaths and give yourselves time to cool down if needed. This helps prevent escalation and fosters a more productive conversation.
2. **Focus on the Issue**: Address the specific issue at hand rather than bringing up past grievances. Staying focused on the present helps keep the conversation constructive.

3. **Seek Solutions Together**: Work collaboratively to find solutions to the conflict. This approach reinforces teamwork and shows that you value your partner's input.

The Role of Non-Verbal Communication

Communication is not solely about words. Non-verbal cues, such as body language, facial expressions, and tone of voice, play a significant role in how messages are received. Being aware of your non-verbal communication can enhance your connection.

- **Maintain Eye Contact**: Eye contact conveys attention and interest. It shows your partner that you are engaged and present in the conversation.
- **Be Mindful of Your Tone**: The tone of your voice can significantly impact how your message is perceived. Strive for a tone that reflects warmth and openness, even during difficult discussions.

Incorporating Faith into Communication

Faith can guide how we communicate with our partners. Reflecting on biblical teachings about love and respect can inspire a healthier approach to conversations.

- **Pray Together**: Before important discussions, consider praying together. Invite God into your conversations, seeking His wisdom and guidance.
- **Reflect on Scripture**: Explore passages that emphasize the importance of love and understanding in communication. Scriptures like James 1:19 remind us to be "quick to listen, slow to speak, and slow to become angry."

Conclusion: The Heart of Connection

Effective communication is the heart of a thriving relationship. By actively listening, expressing needs, and handling conflict with grace, we can nurture our connection and deepen our love. Just as penguins rely on their unique language to stay close, we too must prioritize communication to maintain the warmth and intimacy in our relationships.

In the next chapter, we will explore the significance of shared goals and visions. Together, we'll learn how aligning our dreams can bring us closer and create a future filled with hope and love. Let us embrace the power of communication and continue to build a strong, loving partnership.

Chapter 8: Shared Goals and Visions: Building a Future Together

As penguins journey through the frigid landscape, they not only support each other in daily survival but also work together toward a common goal: raising their young and ensuring the continuation of their species. In our relationships, having shared goals and visions can unify us, providing direction and purpose as we navigate life together.

The Importance of Shared Goals

Shared goals strengthen relationships by fostering teamwork and cooperation. When both partners work toward common objectives, it cultivates a sense of partnership and reinforces the bond of love.

1. **Strengthening Your Connection**: Working toward a shared goal creates opportunities for collaboration, enhancing your connection. It encourages you to rely on each other's strengths and support one another through challenges.
2. **Creating a Sense of Purpose**: Shared goals give your relationship a sense of purpose and direction. They remind you of why you are together and help you navigate the ups and downs of life as a unified team.

Identifying Your Shared Goals

The first step toward building a future together is identifying the goals that matter most to both of you. Here are some key areas to consider:

- **Family Goals**: Discuss your aspirations for family life. Do you envision having children? If so, what kind of upbringing do you hope to provide? Being on the same page about family can strengthen your commitment to one another.

- **Financial Goals**: Talk about your financial aspirations. Do you want to buy a house, save for travel, or invest in your future? Setting financial goals together fosters accountability and encourages open discussions about spending and saving.
- **Personal Growth Goals**: Encourage each other's personal development by discussing individual goals. Whether it's pursuing education, hobbies, or career advancements, supporting each other's dreams enhances your bond.
- **Spiritual Goals**: Aligning your spiritual beliefs and practices can deepen your connection. Consider discussing how you want to grow in faith together, whether through prayer, attending church, or engaging in community service.

Creating a Vision for Your Future

Once you've identified your shared goals, it's time to create a vision for your future together. This vision acts as a guiding light, reminding you of your aspirations and the love that fuels them.

1. **Visualize Your Future**: Take time to visualize what your ideal future looks like. Consider the experiences you want to share, the places you want to visit, and the life you want to build together.
2. **Write It Down**: Documenting your vision can make it more tangible. Create a vision board or write a mission statement for your relationship. This serves as a reminder of your shared dreams and aspirations.
3. **Set Actionable Steps**: Break down your goals into actionable steps. Establish timelines and responsibilities for each partner, ensuring that you both contribute to the journey.

Navigating Challenges Together

As you pursue your shared goals, you may encounter obstacles. Navigating these challenges requires teamwork and resilience.

- **Stay Flexible**: Life is unpredictable. Be open to adjusting your goals and timelines as circumstances change. Flexibility allows you to adapt without losing sight of your shared vision.
- **Communicate Openly**: Maintain open communication as you navigate challenges. Discuss any concerns or frustrations that arise, and work together to find solutions.

Celebrating Milestones Together

As you achieve your shared goals, take the time to celebrate your successes. Acknowledging milestones reinforces the joy of working together and strengthens your bond.

1. **Plan Celebrations**: Whether it's a special dinner, a weekend getaway, or a simple acknowledgment of your progress, celebrating achievements helps you appreciate the journey you've taken together.
2. **Reflect on Your Journey**: Take time to reflect on what you've accomplished and how far you've come. Share your thoughts and feelings about the experience, reinforcing the connection between you.

Faith as a Guiding Principle

Incorporating your faith into your shared goals can provide additional strength and direction. Seek God's guidance as you navigate your aspirations together.

- **Pray for Wisdom**: Regularly pray for wisdom in your decision-making. Invite God into your discussions, asking for His direction as you pursue your dreams.

- **Study Scripture Together**: Explore biblical passages that inspire and encourage you in your journey. Reflecting on God's promises can deepen your faith and enhance your connection.

Conclusion: A Unified Path Forward

Shared goals and visions are essential components of a thriving relationship. By identifying what matters most to both of you and working toward those aspirations, you create a future filled with purpose, love, and unity. Just as penguins thrive in their environment by working together, we too can build a beautiful future through collaboration and commitment.

In the next chapter, we will explore the importance of nurturing romance and intimacy in our relationships. Together, we'll learn how to keep the spark alive and maintain the warmth of love throughout the seasons of life. Let us embrace our shared dreams and continue building a strong, loving partnership.

Chapter 9: Nurturing Romance and Intimacy: Keeping the Spark Alive

As winter fades and spring unfolds, penguins engage in displays of affection, reminding us of the importance of nurturing romance and intimacy in our relationships. Just as these birds rely on their bond to thrive in harsh conditions, we too must prioritize the spark of love that fuels our connection.

The Importance of Romance

Romance is the tender expression of love that enhances emotional intimacy and strengthens the bond between partners. It involves thoughtful gestures, shared experiences, and a deep appreciation for one another.

1. **Rekindling the Flame**: Over time, it's easy for the excitement of romance to fade amid the routines of daily life. Rekindling that flame requires intentional effort, creativity, and a willingness to prioritize each other.
2. **Creating Lasting Memories**: Romantic moments create cherished memories that enrich your relationship. These experiences serve as reminders of your love and commitment, helping to reinforce your connection.

Simple Ways to Foster Romance

Incorporating romance into your daily life doesn't have to be elaborate or costly. Here are some simple yet meaningful ways to nurture romance:

- **Surprise Each Other**: Surprise your partner with small gestures, like leaving a sweet note, preparing their favorite meal, or planning an unexpected date night. These thoughtful acts show your love and consideration.

- **Create Rituals Together**: Establish rituals that you both look forward to. This could be a weekly date night, a morning coffee together, or an evening walk. Consistent quality time strengthens your bond.
- **Express Affection**: Don't underestimate the power of physical affection. Hold hands, give hugs, or share spontaneous kisses. These gestures convey love and reinforce your emotional connection.

Deepening Intimacy

Intimacy goes beyond physical affection; it encompasses emotional, intellectual, and spiritual connection. Deepening intimacy requires openness and vulnerability.

1. **Share Your Thoughts and Feelings**: Create a safe space where both partners feel comfortable sharing their innermost thoughts and feelings. This openness fosters trust and strengthens your emotional bond.
2. **Engage in Deep Conversations**: Set aside time for meaningful conversations. Discuss your dreams, fears, and aspirations. These discussions deepen your understanding of each other and enhance emotional intimacy.
3. **Explore Each Other's Interests**: Take the time to learn about your partner's hobbies and interests. Engaging in activities together fosters connection and demonstrates your commitment to each other's happiness.

Cultivating Spiritual Intimacy

Incorporating your faith into your relationship can enhance intimacy. When you grow spiritually together, you create a deeper bond that transcends the physical.

- **Pray Together**: Regularly pray together, inviting God into your relationship. Sharing prayers and seeking His guidance deepens your connection and fosters a sense of unity.
- **Study Scripture Together**: Explore biblical passages that resonate with your relationship. Discussing and reflecting on these teachings can strengthen your bond and provide insight into your journey together.

Navigating Challenges to Intimacy

As life's pressures mount, maintaining intimacy can be challenging. It's essential to approach these obstacles with understanding and commitment.

- **Prioritize Time Together**: Make a conscious effort to carve out time for each other, even amid busy schedules. Quality time fosters connection and helps you recharge your relationship.
- **Communicate Openly About Needs**: If intimacy wanes, address it openly. Discuss any concerns or desires with compassion, ensuring that both partners feel heard and understood.

Rekindling the Spark During Difficult Times

When challenges arise, it's vital to focus on rekindling the spark in your relationship. Here are some strategies to help you navigate difficult times:

1. **Reflect on Your Love Story**: Take time to reflect on your journey together. Share your favorite memories, milestones, and the

qualities you love most about each other. Reminding yourselves of your shared history can reignite your connection.

2. **Plan a Getaway**: Sometimes, a change of scenery can work wonders. Plan a short trip or staycation to reconnect and create new memories away from everyday stresses.

3. **Engage in New Experiences**: Trying new activities together can reignite excitement in your relationship. Take a dance class, go hiking, or explore a new hobby. New experiences foster intimacy and strengthen your bond.

Conclusion: The Gift of Romance and Intimacy

Nurturing romance and intimacy is essential for a thriving relationship. By prioritizing affectionate gestures, deepening emotional connections, and fostering spiritual intimacy, we can keep the spark of love alive. Just as penguins rely on their bond to thrive in their environment, we too must cultivate our love to weather life's challenges.

As we continue to nurture our romantic connection and intimacy, it's important to remember that love grows gradually, just as it deepens with time and effort. In the next chapter, we will delve into the art of patience—how allowing love to develop slowly and steadily can strengthen your relationship in ways you might not expect. Together, let's learn how to embrace the process of growth and trust in the timing that God has for your love.

Chapter 10: The Art of Patience: Allowing Love to Grow Gradually

In a world that often demands instant results, we can easily forget that true love takes time to mature. It's tempting to look for quick fixes when things aren't going well, or to expect immediate growth after resolving a conflict. However, just as a seed takes time to grow into a strong tree, love requires patience to flourish.

Patience is an essential virtue in every relationship. It's not just about waiting for problems to resolve themselves, but rather, it's about being calm, understanding, and willing to give space for love to grow. Penguins, who patiently endure long winters while protecting and nurturing their eggs, provide us with a beautiful example of how patience is an integral part of sustaining a relationship.

1. Understanding the Timing of Love

God, in His perfect wisdom, has designed everything to happen in its own time. As Ecclesiastes 3:1 says, "For everything there is a season, and a time for every matter under heaven." Relationships are no different. There are seasons when love is full of excitement and joy, and there are seasons when it feels like you're just trying to get through the day. The key is recognizing that every season serves a purpose, and trusting that love will grow stronger through it all.

Just like a penguin pair waits patiently for their egg to hatch, couples must also learn to trust the process. We often expect immediate results in our relationships—whether it's expecting our spouse to change overnight or wanting instant solutions to long-term issues. However, love doesn't work that way. It grows slowly, through moments of grace, forgiveness, and dedication.

2. Allowing Space for Growth

One of the most important aspects of patience is giving each other the space to grow individually and as a couple. We can sometimes be impatient with our partner's flaws or with their pace of personal growth. But we must remember that each person is on their own journey, and growth doesn't happen all at once. Learning to accept this truth and giving each other grace is essential for fostering a healthy, lasting love.

In the same way that penguins protect their young but give them the space to grow and develop naturally, we too must protect our relationships while allowing room for growth. It's about finding the balance between nurturing each other and respecting each other's pace of growth.

3. Persevering Through the Waiting

Patience in love isn't just about waiting—it's about how we wait. There are times in relationships when it feels like things aren't progressing. Maybe you're waiting for trust to be rebuilt, for intimacy to be rekindled, or for wounds to heal. These seasons can feel frustrating and lonely, but they are also opportunities for growth.

Penguins endure harsh winters, huddled together for warmth, waiting for the season to change. They don't rush the process because they understand that time is necessary for survival and growth. In the same way, couples can lean on each other and on God during difficult seasons, trusting that the waiting will produce greater strength and resilience in the relationship.

4. Patience as a Reflection of God's Love

God's love for us is marked by immense patience. He gives us time to grow, to learn, and to become more like Him. As we learn to be patient with our partners, we reflect God's grace and love. Romans 12:12 encourages us to be "joyful in hope, patient in affliction, faithful in prayer." Patience, then, is not just about enduring but about doing so with hope and faith in God's perfect timing.

When we extend patience in our relationships, we are allowing love to take root and grow in a way that is sustainable and enduring. It's a reflection of the way God patiently nurtures His relationship with us, guiding us toward His plan with gentleness and care.

5. Embracing the Journey of Growth

At the heart of patience is the recognition that love is a journey, not a destination. Every step we take in our relationships, whether forward or backward, is part of a larger process. Patience teaches us to embrace the journey, to celebrate the small victories, and to trust that the love we are building will stand the test of time.

Penguins, who mate for life, understand that their relationship is a lifelong commitment. They persevere through difficult conditions because they are in it for the long haul. In the same way, we must approach our relationships with the understanding that love is a marathon, not a sprint. By embracing patience, we allow our love to grow deeper and more meaningful with each passing day.

Conclusion of the Chapter

Patience is not always easy, but it is one of the greatest gifts you can give to your relationship. By embracing the art of patience, you are allowing love to grow gradually, in its own time, and in its own way. Just like the penguins who endure harsh winters together, trusting that the warmth will return, you too can trust that the seeds of love you are nurturing will blossom into something beautiful.

As you cultivate patience in your relationship, remember that it is through waiting, through giving space, and through persevering that true love is able to grow. Trust in God's timing, lean on His grace, and know that, just like the penguins, your love will grow strong and resilient, capable of enduring the seasons of life.

Chapter 11: Nurturing Emotional Connection: The Heart of Love

In the icy landscapes where penguins thrive, their emotional connection is vital for survival. They rely on one another for warmth and support, demonstrating how essential emotional bonds are for enduring life's challenges. In our relationships, nurturing emotional connection is equally crucial for maintaining love and intimacy.

Understanding Emotional Connection

Emotional connection is the deep bond that forms between partners, allowing them to share their thoughts, feelings, and experiences. This connection fosters trust, intimacy, and a sense of belonging.

1. **The Foundation of Love**: An emotional connection is the heartbeat of a healthy relationship. It creates a safe space where both partners feel valued and understood, strengthening their bond.
2. **The Role of Vulnerability**: Being vulnerable with each other is a significant aspect of emotional connection. Sharing fears, dreams, and insecurities fosters intimacy and encourages deeper understanding.

Ways to Strengthen Your Emotional Connection

Building and nurturing your emotional connection requires intentional effort and open communication. Here are some strategies to enhance this vital aspect of your relationship:

1. **Practice Active Listening**: Listening is more than just hearing words; it's about understanding the emotions behind them. Show genuine interest in your partner's thoughts and feelings. Ask open-ended questions and validate their experiences.

2. **Share Your Thoughts and Feelings**: Make it a habit to express your thoughts and feelings regularly. Share your joys, concerns, and daily experiences. This practice deepens your understanding of each other and fosters a sense of partnership.
3. **Engage in Meaningful Conversations**: Set aside time for deeper conversations. Discuss your values, dreams, and aspirations. These discussions create opportunities for emotional connection and help you align your goals.
4. **Be Present**: In our fast-paced world, it's easy to become distracted. Make an effort to be fully present during your interactions. Put away devices and focus on each other, demonstrating that your relationship is a priority.
5. **Show Appreciation**: Regularly express gratitude for your partner. Acknowledge their efforts, qualities, and the love they bring into your life. Simple words of appreciation can go a long way in strengthening your emotional bond.

Navigating Difficult Emotions Together

Emotional challenges are a natural part of any relationship. It's essential to navigate these difficulties together to maintain a strong emotional connection.

1. **Address Conflicts Constructively**: Conflicts are inevitable, but how you address them matters. Approach disagreements with empathy and a desire to understand your partner's perspective. Focus on finding solutions together rather than assigning blame.
2. **Encourage Open Expression**: Create a safe space where both partners feel comfortable expressing their emotions, even difficult ones. Encourage each other to share feelings without fear of judgment.

3. **Practice Patience and Understanding**: Emotions can be complex, and it's essential to be patient with each other during challenging times. Offer support and understanding as you work through difficult feelings together.

The Role of Shared Experiences

Shared experiences play a significant role in strengthening your emotional connection. They create lasting memories and deepen your bond.

1. **Engage in Activities Together**: Participate in activities that both of you enjoy. Whether it's cooking, hiking, or watching movies, shared experiences bring joy and create opportunities for connection.
2. **Celebrate Milestones**: Acknowledge and celebrate important milestones in your relationship, whether they're big or small. These celebrations reinforce your connection and provide opportunities for reflection.
3. **Travel Together**: Exploring new places together can enhance your emotional bond. Traveling allows you to create unique memories and experiences that enrich your relationship.

Incorporating Faith into Your Emotional Connection

Your faith can play a vital role in nurturing your emotional bond. Inviting God into your relationship can deepen your connection and provide guidance.

- **Pray Together Regularly**: Make prayer a regular practice in your relationship. Praying together fosters intimacy and invites God's presence into your lives.

- **Seek God's Guidance**: When navigating emotional challenges, seek God's guidance through prayer and scripture. Reflecting on biblical teachings can provide comfort and direction.

Conclusion: Embracing the Heart of Your Relationship

Nurturing your emotional connection is essential for a thriving relationship. By practicing active listening, expressing feelings, and engaging in meaningful conversations, you can strengthen the bond that unites you. Just as penguins rely on their emotional connections for survival, we too must prioritize this vital aspect of our love.

In the next chapter, we will explore the importance of cultivating a supportive partnership. Together, we'll learn how to lift each other up, navigate challenges, and create a lasting foundation of love and trust. Let us embrace the beauty of our emotional connection as we journey together in our loving partnership.

Chapter 12: Cultivating a Supportive Partnership: Growing Together in Love

In the world of penguins, support is crucial for thriving in harsh conditions. They work together to nurture their young, find food, and navigate their environment. Similarly, a supportive partnership is vital for enduring the ups and downs of life. By cultivating an atmosphere of encouragement and understanding, we can foster a relationship that grows stronger with each challenge we face.

The Essence of a Supportive Partnership

A supportive partnership is built on mutual respect, empathy, and a shared commitment to each other's well-being. It creates a nurturing environment where both partners feel valued and understood.

1. **Emotional Support**: Offering emotional support means being there for each other during tough times. It involves listening, validating feelings, and providing comfort when needed.
2. **Encouragement**: Encourage each other's dreams and aspirations. Celebrate successes, no matter how small, and provide motivation during challenging times. Your belief in each other's potential can make a significant difference.

Building a Foundation of Support

Creating a supportive partnership requires intentional actions and a shared commitment. Here are some strategies to help you cultivate this essential aspect of your relationship:

1. **Communicate Openly**: Effective communication is the cornerstone of a supportive partnership. Share your thoughts, feelings, and needs openly, ensuring that both partners feel heard and understood.

2. **Be Present**: Make a conscious effort to be present for each other. This means actively engaging in conversations, offering a listening ear, and being emotionally available.
3. **Practice Empathy**: Empathy involves understanding and sharing in your partner's feelings. Try to see situations from their perspective, validating their emotions and experiences.
4. **Share Responsibilities**: Support each other by sharing responsibilities in your daily lives. Whether it's household chores, parenting duties, or decision-making, working together fosters teamwork and strengthens your bond.

Navigating Challenges Together

Life is filled with challenges, and how you navigate them as a couple can significantly impact your relationship. Here are some approaches to tackle difficulties together:

1. **Face Challenges as a Team**: Approach challenges as partners, not adversaries. Collaborate on finding solutions and offer support during tough times, reinforcing your commitment to one another.
2. **Seek Compromise**: In disagreements, strive for compromise rather than insisting on being right. This approach fosters collaboration and demonstrates your willingness to prioritize the relationship over individual desires.
3. **Celebrate Resilience**: Acknowledge the challenges you've overcome together. Celebrating your resilience reinforces your bond and reminds you of the strength you possess as a couple.

The Role of Encouragement

Encouragement plays a crucial role in a supportive partnership. By uplifting each other, you create an environment where both partners can thrive.

- **Be Each Other's Cheerleaders**: Regularly express your support for each other's goals and aspirations. Whether it's a new job, a personal project, or a health goal, show enthusiasm and belief in one another.
- **Offer Constructive Feedback**: Providing constructive feedback can help your partner grow and improve. Approach feedback with kindness and understanding, focusing on solutions rather than criticisms.

Faith and Support in Your Partnership

Incorporating your faith into your partnership can deepen your support for one another. Trusting in God's guidance can strengthen your bond and provide comfort during challenging times.

- **Pray for Each Other**: Make it a practice to pray for each other's needs, challenges, and aspirations. Prayer creates a sense of unity and invites God into your relationship.
- **Engage in Faith-Based Activities**: Participate in activities that reinforce your faith together, such as attending church, volunteering, or studying scripture. These shared experiences can enhance your emotional connection.

Conclusion: Embracing a Life of Love and Support

Cultivating a supportive partnership is essential for a thriving relationship. By practicing open communication, empathy, and teamwork, you create a nurturing environment where love can flourish. Just as penguins rely on each other for survival in their harsh environment, we too must cultivate support in our relationships to navigate life's challenges.

As we conclude this chapter, remember that love is a continuous journey of growth and discovery. By nurturing emotional connection, cultivating support, and strengthening trust and mutual respect, you can create a relationship that flourishes. Let us celebrate the love you share and commit to building a strong foundation together as you navigate this beautiful journey of life.

Chapter 13: Strengthening Trust and Mutual Respect in Marriage

Trust and mutual respect are the pillars that hold up any successful and enduring relationship. Without them, even the deepest love can struggle to survive. In the same way that penguins depend on one another to survive in the harshest climates, couples need to build trust and cultivate respect to weather the storms of life together.

Just like the faithfulness of penguins who remain loyal to their partner throughout their lives, trust forms the bedrock of a healthy and vibrant marriage. Trust isn't something that is granted instantly; rather, it is earned over time through consistent actions, open communication, and genuine care for one another. It's about believing that your spouse has your best interests at heart, even in moments of disagreement or hardship.

One of the most important ways to build trust is through honesty. Be transparent with your spouse about your feelings, struggles, and even your dreams. Holding back out of fear or discomfort can lead to misunderstandings that erode the foundation of your relationship. When you are open with your partner, it invites them to trust you more fully and deepens the bond between you.

Respect, on the other hand, means valuing your spouse for who they are, both as an individual and as your partner. It's about recognizing their worth and treating them with kindness, even when you disagree. Respect allows you to see past small irritations and focus on the bigger picture of what makes your partner unique and special. It means appreciating their strengths and being patient with their weaknesses, knowing that no one is perfect, but that love is worth the effort.

The Bible reminds us in Ephesians 5:33 that each husband must love his wife as he loves himself, and the wife must respect her husband. This mutual love and respect are key to cultivating a strong and lasting marriage. When both partners feel valued and trusted, they are more likely to work together through challenges and celebrate successes as a team.

It's also important to remember that trust and respect go hand in hand. Without trust, respect can wane, and without respect, trust can be difficult to maintain. If either is damaged, it can take time and effort to restore. But with God's guidance, healing is always possible. Just as He restores our souls, He can help restore trust and respect in your marriage when both partners commit to the journey of healing and growth.

Practical steps you can take to strengthen trust and respect include:

- **Listen with an open heart**: Make a habit of listening to your spouse without interrupting or immediately offering advice. Sometimes, all they need is for you to hear them out.
- **Honor your promises**: Whether big or small, keeping your promises builds trust over time. When your spouse knows that they can rely on your word, their sense of security in the relationship grows.
- **Show appreciation daily**: Acknowledge the efforts your spouse makes, even the little things. Whether it's a simple "thank you" or a thoughtful gesture, appreciation fosters a culture of respect and kindness in the home.
- **Forgive freely**: No relationship is without its mistakes. When trust is broken, forgiveness is the path to healing. Be quick to forgive, and slow to hold grudges.

In marriage, you are not just partners; you are each other's biggest supporters. Like penguins standing shoulder to shoulder against the icy winds, you and your spouse must stand together, guarding your relationship from the external pressures that seek to pull you apart. With trust, respect, and God at the center, you will find the strength to grow together in love, facing life's challenges with confidence and grace.

In the next chapter, we will explore the beauty of sacrifice in marriage—how putting your partner first can deepen your connection and bring you closer to the love that God designed for you both.

Chapter 14: The Gift of Sacrifice: Putting Your Partner First

One of the greatest acts of love that we can offer in marriage is the gift of sacrifice. It may seem counterintuitive at first—after all, why should we give up something we want for the sake of someone else? But when we look at the example of true love, as modeled by Christ, we see that sacrifice is not just an occasional act, but a way of life. It's an essential part of building a relationship that reflects God's love and grows stronger over time.

Just as penguins are willing to endure hardship and share their resources with their mate and young, so too must couples learn the art of putting one another first. Sacrifice in marriage isn't about giving up everything you enjoy or losing your sense of self. Instead, it's about placing the needs and happiness of your spouse at the forefront of your heart and actions.

In John 15:13, we read, "Greater love has no one than this: to lay down one's life for one's friends." While this passage points to the ultimate sacrifice Christ made for us, it also applies to our everyday relationships. Sacrificing for your spouse doesn't mean laying down your life in a literal sense, but it does mean laying down your preferences, pride, or desires for the sake of your spouse's wellbeing and the health of your marriage.

The Power of Small Sacrifices

Sacrifice doesn't always have to be grand gestures. In fact, it's often the small, daily sacrifices that build the foundation of trust and love in a marriage. Perhaps you choose to listen attentively even when you're tired, or you decide to spend time doing something your spouse enjoys rather than focusing on your own interests. These little acts of love, over time, show your spouse that they are valued and loved.

Consider how a penguin takes turns caring for its egg with its mate. One partner stands guard, braving the cold for long hours, while the other goes in search of food. Each is sacrificing their comfort and energy for the sake of the family's survival. Similarly, in a marriage, it's the willingness to step outside of your comfort zone for the sake of your spouse that creates an unbreakable bond.

Putting Your Partner First

Sacrificing for your spouse means putting their needs above your own. This doesn't mean neglecting yourself or ignoring your personal growth, but rather ensuring that in the decisions you make and the actions you take, your spouse's happiness and wellbeing are taken into account.

For example, if your spouse is feeling overwhelmed with responsibilities, offering to help or share the burden can be a powerful act of love. Whether it's taking on more household tasks or being emotionally available during tough times, these sacrifices reflect a deep commitment to the partnership.

When both partners adopt this mindset—mutually putting one another first—it creates a cycle of giving and receiving that strengthens the marriage. Rather than focusing on what you can get from the relationship, the focus shifts to what you can give. And in giving, you often receive far more in return.

The Beauty of Selflessness

Selflessness is a key ingredient to making any relationship thrive, and in marriage, it's essential. It's about learning to let go of the "me" mentality and embracing the "we" mindset. As we see in Philippians 2:3-4, "Do nothing out of selfish ambition or vain conceit. Rather, in humility value others above yourselves, not looking to your own interests but each of you to the interests of the others." When we live selflessly, our hearts become more open, and love flows more freely.

This doesn't mean you should neglect your own needs or become a martyr in your relationship. Healthy sacrifice is about balance—finding ways to support and love your spouse without losing sight of your own worth and wellbeing. It's not about doing everything for your spouse, but about willingly sharing the load and being present when they need you most.

The Ultimate Example of Sacrificial Love

The greatest example of sacrificial love is found in Jesus Christ. He gave everything for us, even to the point of death on the cross. His love was unconditional, not based on what we could offer Him but on His deep desire to restore and redeem us. When we follow this example in our marriages, we begin to experience a deeper and more fulfilling connection with our spouse.

Sacrificial love mirrors the love that God has for us. When we willingly lay down our pride, our desires, or even our time for the sake of our spouse, we are living out the love that God designed for marriage. It is a love that builds bridges, heals wounds, and strengthens the bond between husband and wife.

How to Practice Sacrificial Love Daily:

- **Be intentional**: Make a habit of looking for small ways to serve your spouse. Whether it's making them coffee in the morning or giving them a break from the kids, these little gestures go a long way.
- **Be patient**: Sometimes sacrifice requires patience, especially when your spouse is going through a difficult time. Stay committed to supporting them, even when it's not easy.

- **Communicate**: Talk with your spouse about what they need or what would help them feel more supported. Open dialogue is key to understanding how you can serve each other better.
- **Celebrate your spouse**: Acknowledge the sacrifices your spouse makes for you. Gratitude and recognition can fuel even more love and support in your marriage.

As you grow together in sacrificial love, you will find that your marriage becomes a reflection of God's perfect love—one that is selfless, enduring, and deeply fulfilling. Together, you can weather any storm, just like penguins standing side by side in the cold, knowing that your love is strong enough to withstand the challenges that life may bring.

In the final chapter, we will explore how being anchored in God's love provides the unshakable foundation for a marriage that endures and flourishes through every season of life.

Chapter 15: Anchored in God's Love: The Unshakable Foundation for a Lasting Relationship

As we've journeyed through the many aspects of nurturing love and commitment in a marriage, it becomes clear that there is one source of love that never falters, never fades, and never grows cold: God's love. While human love, even in the strongest of marriages, can face trials, disappointments, and seasons of struggle, God's love remains steadfast. It is an anchor for our souls and a foundation upon which we can build lasting relationships that endure the test of time.

When we place our trust in God, we open ourselves to a love far greater than anything we could experience on our own. His love is the very source from which we can draw strength, wisdom, and grace to love our spouse in ways that reflect His heart. In Romans 5:5, it says, *"God's love has been poured out into our hearts through the Holy Spirit, who has been given to us."* This love, poured into our hearts, is what equips us to love our partner even in the toughest seasons.

The Nature of God's Love

God's love is unlike any other. It's not based on feelings or fleeting emotions but is rooted in His very nature. God is love (1 John 4:8), and everything He does flows from that essence. His love is unconditional, meaning it is not dependent on our actions, worthiness, or performance. In the same way, when we allow God's love to flow through us, we can love our spouse without expecting anything in return.

This kind of love is the antithesis of the world's view of love, which often focuses on what one can get rather than what one can give. But in a marriage grounded in God, we begin to understand that love is about serving, sacrificing, and giving of ourselves, just as Christ gave

Himself for us. When both partners are anchored in God's love, they find a deeper connection with one another, sustained not by their own strength but by the endless reservoir of God's grace.

The Strength to Endure

Life will inevitably bring seasons of difficulty—whether it's the stress of financial pressures, health challenges, or simply the daily grind of managing responsibilities. In those moments, it's easy for love to cool, for distance to grow, and for frustration to build. But God's love provides the strength to endure. His love doesn't change with circumstances; it remains constant and true.

Just as penguins endure harsh winters, huddling together for warmth and survival, a couple can weather life's storms by leaning into God's love. When we trust in Him, we find the resilience to push through the difficult times. His love empowers us to offer grace, forgiveness, and patience when it seems impossible to do so on our own.

In Ephesians 3:17-19, Paul prays that we may be "rooted and established in love, [so that we] may have power, together with all the Lord's holy people, to grasp how wide and long and high and deep is the love of Christ." This love, which surpasses knowledge, is the very foundation that enables a marriage to thrive.

Unconditional Love: A Reflection of God's Heart

Human love often comes with conditions—whether spoken or unspoken. We may love our spouse as long as they meet certain expectations or behave in ways that we deem acceptable. But God's love for us is radically different. He loves us not because of what we do but because of who He is. And when we experience that unconditional love, we are empowered to love our spouse in the same way.

In marriage, reflecting God's love means choosing to love our spouse even when they fall short, make mistakes, or disappoint us. It means extending grace and forgiveness as Christ has extended them to us. This kind of love isn't based on what we receive but on what we are willing to give.

The beauty of unconditional love is that it creates a safe space in the marriage for both partners to grow, learn, and become more like Christ. It fosters an environment of trust, security, and deep connection, where both individuals know that they are loved for who they are, not just for what they do.

The Role of the Holy Spirit in Our Marriage

It's important to remember that we don't have to love in our own strength. As Romans 5:5 reminds us, God's love has been poured into our hearts by the Holy Spirit. This means that we have a constant source of divine love flowing through us, enabling us to love our spouse in ways that go beyond our human capacity.

When we rely on the Holy Spirit, we are able to love selflessly, forgive freely, and give generously. The Holy Spirit empowers us to be patient when we are tempted to be frustrated, to speak words of life when we want to complain, and to act with kindness even when we feel wronged. Through the Holy Spirit, we are equipped to reflect God's perfect love in our imperfect human relationships.

Building a Marriage that Lasts

Ultimately, a marriage anchored in God's love is a marriage that lasts. When we make Him the foundation of our relationship, we can face any challenge with confidence, knowing that we are not alone. His love strengthens us, sustains us, and guides us through every season of life.

As you reflect on the journey of building a lasting marriage, remember that God's love is the key. It is the unshakable foundation upon which you can build a relationship that not only survives but thrives. When we place our trust in Him, we receive the power to love in ways that are beyond ourselves—ways that reflect His heart and His plan for marriage.

As we conclude this journey together, may you be reminded that love is not just an emotion; it's a choice, a commitment, and a reflection of God's grace. Through His love, you can cultivate a marriage that is strong, enduring, and full of joy. Trust in His love, lean on His strength, and allow His Spirit to guide your hearts as you continue to grow together in the beautiful gift of marriage.

Conclusion: The Everlasting Flame of Love

As we reach the end of this journey through the intricacies of love and partnership, it's essential to reflect on the foundation that can sustain and invigorate our relationships: the love of God. Throughout the chapters, we have explored how forgiveness, emotional connection, and support form the pillars of a thriving relationship. However, it is the divine love of God that truly empowers us to overcome the challenges we face and keeps our hearts ablaze, even in the coldest of times.

The Foundation of Divine Love

Human love, while beautiful, is often susceptible to the trials of life. Misunderstandings, external pressures, and even our own shortcomings can lead to moments where love feels cold or distant. Yet, the love that God offers is unwavering and unconditional. It is a love that transcends human limitations, providing a source of strength that we can draw from in every circumstance.

As Romans 5:5 reminds us, "God's love has been poured into our hearts through the Holy Spirit." This divine love fills us with a warmth and security that cannot be diminished by the trials we encounter. When we put our trust in God, we invite His perfect love into our relationships, enabling us to love one another in a way that reflects His grace.

The Power of Trusting in God

Trusting in God means surrendering our fears, insecurities, and past hurts to Him. It allows us to approach our partners with renewed hope and a deeper capacity to forgive and heal. As we cultivate a relationship with God, we discover that His love empowers us to extend that same love to others, creating a cycle of grace and understanding.

In times of struggle, we can turn to God for guidance and strength. By praying together and inviting Him into our relationship, we strengthen the bond that ties us. His presence can transform our love, keeping it vibrant and resilient.

A Love that Endures

The love of God is not merely a backdrop for our relationships; it is the very essence that fuels them. When we anchor our love in His promises, we find a foundation that withstands the storms of life. The trials we face become opportunities for growth rather than reasons for separation.

This divine love teaches us that true intimacy is rooted in vulnerability, trust, and mutual support. It encourages us to embrace one another's imperfections and celebrate our shared journey. In doing so, we mirror the steadfastness of God's love—a love that never cools, never falters, and always seeks to uplift.

Final Thoughts

As you continue your journey in love, remember that the most profound connections are built on the unshakeable foundation of God's love. By allowing His love to permeate your hearts, you equip yourselves with the tools needed to navigate life's challenges together.

Let this love be the flame that never goes out, the warmth that drives away the coldness, and the light that guides your path. Together, with God as your cornerstone, you can experience a love that is not just enduring but transformative—one that reflects the beauty of His grace and mercy.

Embrace this journey with faith, knowing that as you cultivate love rooted in God, you are not only building a relationship that thrives but also participating in a divine narrative of love that echoes through eternity.

Credits

Rekindling Love: Lessons from Penguins and Faith to Restore Your Marriage By Albert Barzaga

Author Note: Albert Barzaga is a pen name for Ramón Alberto Bárzaga Sánchez.

Acknowledgments: I am profoundly grateful to God for the wisdom and guidance that inspired and enabled me to create and design this book. Your divine support has been a source of strength and creativity throughout this journey.

Thank you for reading this book. For more updates and content, follow me on Pinterest: https://www.pinterest.com/pastoralbertbarzaga